KINGDOM AND WISDOM'S PARABLES

KINGDOM AND WISDOM'S PARABLES

ALDIVAN TORRES

Canary Of Joy

Contents

1 Kingdom and Wisdom's Parables   1

I

Kingdom and Wisdom's Parables

"Kingdom and Wisdom's Parables"
Aldivan Teixeira Torres

Author: Aldivan Teixeira Torres
©2018-Aldıvan Teixeira Torres
All the rights reserved
Aldivan Teixeira Torres

This book, including all its parts, is protected by copyright and don't can to be reproduced without author's permission, resold or transferred.

Short Biography: Aldivan Teixeira Torres, born in Brazil, develops the series of novels "the seer", poetry, books of the genre self-help, religious, the field of wisdom, among others. To date, it has published titles in Portuguese, Spanish, English, French, and Italian. From an early age, he has always been a lover of the art of writing and has consolidated a professional career since the second semester of 2013. He hopes to contribute to the Pernambuco and Brazilian culture, arousing the pleasure of reading in those who do not have the habit. Your mission is to win the heart of each of your readers. Besides literature, his main tastes are music, travel, friends, family and the very pleasure of living. "For literature, equality, fraternity, justice, dignity, and honor of the human being always" is his motto.

Introduction

The Kingdom and Wisdom's parables are a collection of parables that have as purpose the instruction for diverse situations that occur in our life. Let us look for in these parables the thread that unrolls in the midst of our problems, and we will live better.

I hope that they contribute in some way to the life of the readers and if at least one person is satisfied with this book, I will give a good use of the time used in their making. A hug.

The author
Kingdom and Wisdom's Parables
Introduction
The firstborn and the bastard
The Black Knight
The Black Knight: Meaning
The true friend
The true friend (meaning)
The two employees
The two employees (meaning)
The great apple trees
The great apple tree (meaning)
The humble and the proud
The parable of the foolish man
The plantation
The Barn and The Cobra
The two commoners

Parable of Creation
The kingdom
The true victory
The merchant and the consumer
The two shepherds
The rich boy and the poor boy
The Alien and the Earth man
The Labyrinth
The Game of Life
The Fish and the Star
The Invisible Companion
The Drunk And the conscious
The antiquarian
The Librarian
Forewarned and reckless
The key
The frog and the butterfly
An Important Lesson
Parable of life

The firstborn and the bastard

Joshua was a prosperous merchant in Recife. He was married and had two children named Abelardo and Roger. Abelard was his son with his legitimate wife, and Roger was the fruit of an extramarital relationship. The two were raised together and treated equally by their parents. When they grew up, they learned the truth that they were half-brothers. Initially, this did not affect the relationship of the two, with them accepting a good one. However, over time, the firstborn (Abelard) began to implicate his half-brother; therefore, he always wanted more attention from parents than did not happen.

With the opening of two more stores, Joshua decided to call a family meeting to declare his decision. The children attended, and their father began the dialogue.

"My children, we are gathered here to deliberate on an important question: The administration of the new stores that I have just inaugurated. I'm already very busy with the ones I have, and so I'm going to pass them on to my two children. Each of you will have a store. I am not discriminating against anyone because they both have the same sales capacity. What do they tell me? Accepted?

The eldest son rose angrily and protested:

"Is not fair. I have the right to stay with the two stores because I am your true son, the fruit of true love. While there, it's just an error.

The father, disgusted, broke out on top of him and slapped him.

"You are the one who has no right to humiliate you." He is my son as much as you are. What is mine, do what I want. By this attitude, I will take away the administration from the store and deliver this to my other son because he did not even open his mouth to complain about my decision. Whoever deserves it will be given even more.

The Black Knight

There was, in a distant kingdom, an excellent and powerful king. He was served by numerous faithful servants who loved him. Each day, he chose some more to grow his wheat field because he was huge. Among the workers, there was one named Angel, who was one of the most important servants. He had six talents of significant importance. However, he did not know how to handle these tools and did not want to hurt others. The king, all powerful, knew of his acts because of the damage he was causing. At every turn of his, the king paid a gigantic sum in compensation to his creditors. The time passed and Angel unknowingly continued sowing tares instead of wheat. The king loved him. Among the servants, there was no one above him. However, the king realized that if he did not take an energetic attitude, he would ruin the plantation and with that, he would be sentenced to prison no matter how much it hurt him. Then the king decided to send the black knight.

The black knight, also called the devastating plague, was the first evil known in his field. He is the father of lies and malice. He approached Angel and began to cry:

"The weeds that you have unwittingly sowed I will gather you now. On the way back, I come to pick you up, too.

In this, a white knight appeared and complemented:

"This is just a warning. If you continue to carry out your crimes you will also be condemned as was this tare. The king sent me here to alert you. He knows you sowed tares thinking it was wheat. That is why he spared him this plague. Now, continue your work and be careful not to sow more tares.

At this moment, Angel had proof of the true love you had for him. From that day on, he would mend and cultivate the harvest more quickly.

The Black Knight: Meaning

The king represents the creator. The subjects represent their creatures. Wheat is the world. Tools are the talents that God gives us when we are born. An angel is a higher spirit sent by God to enlighten the world. Because of his gift, he sometimes harmed his fellow men. The king treats him as a son and therefore forgives his slips. The energetic attitude represents the celestial force that clarifies the true path of good. The black knight is the forces of evil that try in every possible way to harm the servants of the highest. The white knight represents the heavenly guardians who protect the spirits of light. Moral of the parable: God is always willing to give a second chance to those who recognize their mistakes.

The true friend

Gilson, Humberto, and Ronald were inseparable friends. The three of them had known each other since they had studied elementary education. He spent his childhood, came to youth and remained friends. They got married and although the weather got shorter, they continued to be seen on weekends. Occasionally, the three of them would go out alone when the program they were going to enjoy was only suitable for men: games, fishing, adventure tours. One weekend, they combined a boat trip in the surroundings of the beautiful *Angra dos Reis*. They prepared everything: They prepared a nice barbecue, took some caipirinhas and a lot of soda. In addition, they brought with them a powerful sound system to perform some samba classics. The party was hectic and the party too. In this shuttle, Gilson approached the end of the boat without realizing it because the weather was cloudy and the fog began to thicken, making it impossible for him to see clearly where they were. The party's pace slowed, and they decided to rest a little. Plumb! The noise of something falling into the water and the shrill scream of someone caught the attention of everyone. It was Gilson: A slipping unbalanced him and his body was thrown under the waters. I cannot swim! She screamed.

Humberto pondered and said, "I do not know how to swim, either." I'm not going to risk it because I have children to raise.

Ronald felt himself shudder inside and was moved by his colleague's situation. He said, "I do not know how to swim, either. However, he is my friend and I will not leave him alone in this difficult situation.

Another noise: Plumb! Ronaldo threw himself into the stormy waters to help him. Wrapped in haze, he shouted his name to locate him. Something cleared his way and found Gilson almost exhausted and unable to swim. When Gilson saw him, he exclaimed, "You should not have come." I know you do not swim either. We're going to succumb together!

Ronald replied, "I do not care. Do you remember how you helped me in that desperate financial crisis? My family and I are grateful until now. We owe your life. Because of this and the person you are, I do not mind losing you if you have to.

Ronald embraced Gilson and gave him all the reserve power he had. This made him resist for a while longer. Exhausted by exhaustion, they drowned, when suddenly a mighty hand held them up. We are saved! They both shouted with happiness. They were on a small boat guided by a strange man who had not shown up. Furthermore, they both questioned him. Where did you come from? Who are you? How did you find us? The strange guide exclaimed, "So many questions!" The important thing is that you are well. Well, my name is Pedro, and I'm a fisherman. I was fishing in this area and I found you almost drowning. They were not to enter the sea without the skill of swimming. It's very dangerous. Gilson and Ronald again embrace and thank the heavens for being alive. Peter commented: Your friendship is what saved you. I'm not here because I want to and because they sent me. I'm just steering the boat. Furthermore, I did not save them. The hand that pulled them out of the water was the same one that once pulled me. With him, I learned the true meaning of what it is to be a true friend: He gave his life to save us. He told me he would do it all over again if necessary. He is the way, the truth, and the life. Keep it up, friends, like you are today. Let intrigue and envy never scatter them. Remember: Those who seek to protect their life will lose it. But whoever loses it for love will find it. You have been given a new opportunity: Go home and believe in Jesus Christ.

A numbness fell on them and when they awoke, they were on dry land. They got up without really understanding why they were there. Their memories were erased and the only thing they felt was that their friendship was capable of withstanding the stormy fury of the waters.

The true friend (meaning)

The fog is all that disrupts a relationship. Falling in the water are the stumbling blocks we have in our lives. Ronald is the faithful friend who is capable of anything to help the other. In the end, the union of the two overcomes the difficulties.

The two employees

Jesse was a wealthy landlord who employed many servants in his undertakings. Among his enterprises, the most profitable was the vineyard. In one of them, two servants cultivated the same land space: Daniel and Lamuel. Daniel was a dedicated servant who cultivated It was sown, fertilized, and irrigated at the right time. Lamuel was disobedient and foolish because he only followed his convictions: He sowed the grains in a disorderly and unthinking way, fertilized excessively and did not irrigate the seedlings. Daniel thrived and thrived, which earned him praise from his master. Lamuel's field was fruitless. The master called Lamuel and rebuked him for his conduct and advised him to follow Daniel's example. He felt humiliated and displeased at his companion Daniel, decided to take revenge.

The first attitude he took was to ally himself with the master's chief enemy: The chief of the servants who had rebelled against him. He would serve as an instrument of hatred for this evil to destroy all that Daniel had built and conquered, beyond of damaging the plantation of the boss. The enemy gave him a plague, that he entered the field of his companion. Meanwhile, Daniel continued with his work without distrusting of anything. Shortly after, the beautiful green of its field was disappearing, which caused him some surprise and disappointment. With this, he appeared before the chief to provide clarification.

"Sir, I continue to cultivate the soil in the same way. However, what once produced innumerable fruits now produces practically none? I think I'm getting useless. If you wish, I will give my place to another, more competent servant.

"No need, good servant. It was not your fault. I will know what is happening: Your field is being attacked by a powerful plague. An enemy sowed him. But he will not win. I will give you my best insecticide and your field will again give good and beautiful fruits.

The insecticide was applied, and the plague was suppressed. But Lamuel did not give up his revenge. He consulted his master and he promised to destroy Daniel's life and career. In the end, evil became incarnate and took human form: a buyer. Daniel remained obedient and, in his work, honored his boss. The buyer came up and asked, "Are you Daniel? I have heard very well of you. They say that you are the boss's best employee. Daniel politely replied, "I am only a humble servant and equal to everyone. Since I came here, my sole purpose is to fulfill my function. My boss puts all confidence in me and therefore does not I can disappoint you. Come on, I'll show you what I've cultivated so far.

The buyer was led among the beautiful vines of Daniel's field. The buyer exclaimed, "Excellent! You did an impressive job. Tell me, boy, did not you want to work for me? I would give you a generous pay. Daniel replied:

"No, thank you. I do not do this for the money. My reward is all the fruits I reap.

The buyer looked at him with pure hatred and decided to take advantage of Daniel being alone to try to destroy his plantation. He changed his appearance, and no one knows where he got a scythe. He shouted, "Look what I do with your work, look!" (He began to reap Daniel's plans.) When he had finished ravaging the camp, he began to beat him. The master observed everything and decided to act: He called his strongest servant (No one is so brave as to challenge him) and ordered:

"Miguel, go and deliver my servant Daniel, for he is being beaten by the serpent. As for the other plague, let me handle it.

The angel flew hastily toward the field and was armed to the teeth. He seized the ancient serpent, chained it and threw it into the abyss where it could no longer leave (except with permission). Daniel was injured, but he would recover from his injuries. The master summoned Lamuel and he stood before him.

The lord said: "You poison!" Who taught you to act this way? Did you think you were going to destroy my son? Neither you nor the enemy can with him. I am always on the side of the wronged. Instead of envying you because it does not work, done it? I would have blessed him too. Because you rebelled and for your crimes, I no longer want you in my plantation. It will be tied up and thrown into the outer darkness made of weeds that is useless. There will be weeping and gnashing of teeth.

The two employees (meaning)

The landlord is God Himself. The parable presents two servants: one obedient and one disobedient. Daniel acts in the way God expects of a servant: He sows the word of the kingdom, he nurses the newborn plants so that they grow and in the balance of accounts, the boss praises Daniel's attitudes but disapproves of Lamuel's that instead of following the example of the companion, he prefers to harm him. This attitude is very common: People who adopt this way of life feel wronged by God and the world and do not recognize when they are wrong. However, God protects the oppressed and does not allow the servants dedicated to him to be destroyed. In the end, God performs justice and frees from all evil.

The great apple trees

In a garden full of fruit trees there was a large apple tree. It was the most beautiful and leafy tree in the orchard. Every year, the harvest increased and the lord profits from the garden as well. The gardener irrigated twice a day: One with fresh water and another with brackish water. The harvest continued to be full, but gradually the profits were diminishing because some fruits were spoiling before being harvested. Over time, the income from the extraction of the fruits no longer compensated to maintain it. Then the gardener decided to speak with the lord of the garden about the apple tree.

"Dad, I'm thinking of cutting the apple tree because the crop is ruining. What do you say to me?

"Before any decision, I have to see her. It may be that the problem has a solution.

Upon analyzing it, the boss found that all the fruits were spoiling, minus one of the medium. He felt his trunk and touched him,

"Not the court." This is a good tree that has already given me much joy. The apples are spoiling because they are absorbing brackish water instead of sweet. See that fruit of the middle: it is perfect. This is a sign that she protected him by making him absorb only fresh water. By this fruit, which is kept whole, I will not bring it down.

The great apple tree (meaning)

The apple tree represents the life concretely expressed in creation. The harvest is all those good produces life. Fresh water is the word of God and the ways to fulfill it. Brackish water is all contrary directions to the word. Fruits rotten are all those who deviate from the true path of God: love and serve the neighbor. The fruit of the environment is the small contingent that believes and follows the precepts of good without looking back. Even if there is only one faithful, God will bless the land on his behalf.

The humble and the proud

In a large field, full of fruit trees and plantations, there were two servants: Joshua and Jeroboam. They cultivated the field and tended the flock of the boss's sheep. Joshua was a lieutenant and obedient to God, reserving himself to do his work. Jeroboam, on the contrary, boasted of his innumerable talents and sought to seduce the sheep so that they would follow him. Jeroboam's pride grew in such a way that he declared himself the son of his master. To assume the throne and the power that did not belong to him. Then the boss decided to summon him to introduce himself. He said:

"I heard you call yourself, my son. Who gave you such authority? Do you want to match me?

"Revive my being of such splendorous glory that I have come to be your beloved son. I know you've hidden this secret from everyone. Now, I want my share in the inheritance.

"You're crazy. You are not my son. I only have one son: the firstborn. I will give him the throne and the power. If you were my son, I would not be so proud. Despite having created everything and everyone and having the universe in the palm of my hands, I do not count advantages. My works are those who speak for me. In addition to my pupil, I adopted several of my employees for being faithful. A living example is Joshua. He recognizes my authority and accomplishes the work that, for this, I declare today, "He is my son as well. I have begot him. And further, He that humbled himself shall be exalted, and he that exalted himself shall be humbled."

The parable of the foolish man

The master gathered his disciples to the seashore, and a great multitude gathered around him. The master holds all the secrets of the universe and was sent to the lost sheep. However, he spoke to them in parables so that the "blind" and "deaf" did not understand. These had their hearts and minds closed, and so they did not understand what he was saying. On the other hand, those committed to the kingdom could see in their teachings the true path. Then he began to teach: Behold, a foolish man can be likened to a ship that gradually sinks into the high seas. With every transgression committed, a chamber is flooded, and with it a host of good feelings and virtues is shipwrecked., vices) begin to exert a strong oppression on him and consequently the acts harmful to the neighbor and himself become more frequent. On the contrary, the angels (the good intentions and acts) begin to weaken and are forgotten in his life. At an unconscious moment, the angels seek in a last effort to make him see the way to restore balance and union between the creator and the creature. But defects act and prevent the regeneration of man because they are forceful. When all compartments are flooded and salvation is already impossible according to man, the father can perform the miracle. But, for that, it takes surrender, confidence, repentance and the sincere intent of change for the fool.

The plantation

There were, somewhere in the world, three farmers who decided to join together to take care of a plantation together and, consequently, aim at a good crop. To achieve this, they decided to divide their tasks to achieve their objectives and to achieve a perfect synchronization between the third one sowed and planted the seedlings. This year there was adequate sun and rain and the plantation thrived. The three were happy to see their work rewarded. The first farmer said, "I deserve at least half of the profits because if I did not prepare the land with such care, we would not have a large harvest as "If I had not dug the ground with such precision, the plants would not grow that way. Soon, I deserve most of the harvest." The third disagreed: — I do not accept the proposal of either of you. I must remember that if I did not show correctly the number of seeds and their disposition, we would have a derisory harvest. In addition, the seedlings that I planted were the ones that fruited more. Therefore, I deserve to be with the greatest as they did not decide, they decided to call a neighboring plantation to settle the question. "Who would have the right to most of the harvest? The neighbor asked, who prepares the land? The first, proud, rumbled Tell me, is it not me who has more merit to demand the greater part of the profit? The referee remained silent. This time he asked, who dug the ground?

The second, super happy, said: "It was me! You see that you have intelligence enough to realize that I am most responsible for this harvest.

The referee remained silent. Finally, he asked, "Who sowed the seeds and planted the seedlings?" The third shouted, "It was me! Do you see that harvest beauty? There would be nothing without my work.

The referee reflected a little and then said, "I see that none of you alone would get this result. Each one of you with your art contributed decisively to that. I do not see among the three more important or more arduous work that deserves most of the profits. See the ants and the bees and learn. The cooperative work is that builds something and everyone should enjoy their results evenly. Stop arguing and be fair. Take advantage of this harvest because the worker has the right to his salary at the right moment when he reaps the fruits.

The Barn and The Cobra

Behold, there was a wealthy man in a distant kingdom. He owned innumerable properties and animals, besides dozens of employees.

Among them was one that stood out: Xerxes, the general manager of his business. Extremely faithful and attentive to his employer, he was zealous for his interests.

Most of the servants worked in the great cornfield growing the most diverse cereals for own consumption, of the boss and for sales. It was a type of lease: they paid a certain amount per area to the owner. Another part of the servants took care of the most varied types of cattle of the boss. They received a salary for their work. They were happy and quiet with their respective families. "Sometimes serving someone does not characterize suffering, slavery, or humiliation. It should be remembered that Christ came to serve, even as a king. "A few servants served their lord directly in the main headquarters of their estates, where there was a large barn attached. In this was kept all his treasure: Jewels, gold, stones possession documents and large quantities of grain. Beside the house there was also a large corral where all herds were kept. The servants of the house were the most esteemed and had the greatest confidence of the master. They had free access to the barn and to the corral, mainly Xerxes, the aforementioned manager. Being feared and powerful, the boss never considered the possibility of being robbed.

One day, the boss traveled to a nearby town because he had been invited to attend a large wedding party. As usual, he let his employee Xerxes take care of everything. The one who had secretly already convinced two of his subordinates to help him on a plane. And what better time to put it into practice than in his absence? Xerxes was the kind of fake employee. He liked the boss in exchange for his favors. For him, position, money, and power were the only things that mattered. "The others were just useful objects to achieve their aspirations." First, Xerxes sent one of his partners looking for mules, these would serve to remove all the cereal from the barn. Another went after a cattle buyer, to empty the corral of the boss. The other servants of the house did not notice anything because they had been dismissed by Xerxes. The other goods were taken personally by him. "The key to the boss's barn was made available to everyone who lived in the house because they lived in his heart, and this was the key." The mules arrived, the buyer of cattle and the bad servants, too. They took everything they could and distributed the spoils. After the illicit operation, Xerxes and the employees left.

The next day, returning from the trip, the master was shocked to realize the desolation that hung on his property: The corral was empty, and the barn door was broken into. Everything he owned had been taken away. As he entered the house, he saw the furniture turned upside down and some broken. On the floor he saw a small note, which he hurried to collect. In it, Xerxes clarified the fact: The headquarters employees had rebelled, and he took it surprised, could not contain the mutiny. Everything had been stolen. After the thieves left, they hired men to follow them. In the end, he apologized and resigned because he found himself incompetent in his duties. At the end of the letter, the master burst into tears. The sense of injustice, of betrayal, and of repentance filled his thoughts. As a boss and as a citizen, he felt dignified and honest. Why then had he been betrayed? Just him who had full confidence in his employees. A cruel world was where people took advantage of the good faith of others naiver. Moreover, you would still have to pay a mortgage for a loan with a lender. Desolation took over everything that was there.

Feeling ruined, he remembered how far he had departed from God: Misinformed in prayer; In his attitudes, he had not placed his will in the foreground and clung to material goods which were neither the way nor the essence of salvation. "In the bad moments, the human being is changed to question and to seek in a higher being the miraculous solution of his problems". We forget the responsibility for our actions, which have consequences. Taken with anguish and emotion, he knelt down and prayed earnestly that the robbery be cleared up (the Xerxes version had not completely convinced him). On the night of that same day, the Lord of the heavens had compassion and sent a dream: In him, Xerxes, he became a snake and bit him. His mind unraveled the riddle of the robbery, but his heart refused to believe it. Xerxes was seen by him as a son. Feeling ruined, he remembered how far he had departed from God: Misinformed in prayer; In his attitudes, he had not placed his will in the foreground and clung to material goods which were neither the way nor the essence of salvation. "In the bad moments, the human being is changed to question and to seek in a higher being the miraculous solution of his problems". We forget the responsibility for our actions, which have consequences. Taken with anguish and emotion, he knelt down and prayed earnestly that the robbery be cleared up (the Xerxes version had not completely convinced him). On the night of that same day, the Lord of the heavens had compassion and sent a dream: In him, Xerxes, he became a snake and bit him. His mind unraveled the riddle of the robbery, but his heart refused to believe it. Xerxes was seen by him as a son.

At dawn, the employees came in normally for the day of service. They were astonished at what they saw: The property had been ransacked. Seeing them, the boss did not believe: How could they be so cynical? How dare they appear on your property? He received them rather roughly:

"You rascals, what are you doing here?" Did you come here to steal your clothes too?

One of them protested:

"What is it, boss?" We are not responsible for theft. We would be incapable of it. The day before yesterday, we were off-duty. Xerxes freed us.

A snap woke him up from the trance in which he was making him notice Xerxes's sordid plot. The dream he had had been fully deciphered. Then he said:

"Good employees, I cannot keep you here. I do not have enough for that. When I rise, I will give the fair share of their services. At the moment, they are excused.

However, they replied: However, they replied:

"We are staying. As for salary, do not worry: We will work only in exchange for food. We will not abandon you at this difficult time in your life.

Emotion stirred his soul and he cried:

"As of today, you are no longer my employees. Most of all, they are my friends because they consoled me when I was sad, they fed me when

I was hungry, they gave me water when I was thirsty, and they supported me when I was alone. Come, my brothers, come into my house, into my life and into my kingdom.

The two commoners

There were once in Galatia two peasants, Abimael and Josiah. The first had a vineyard on a plot of land leased for that purpose. The landlord who had leased it was the ruler of the area. In the second, he worked as an employee of one of Galatia's most important squatters. His dream was to own a plot of land and plant a vineyard. They were both friends, but they had not seen each other for a long time.

The ruler of Galatia had a daughter of the name of Jerusa, 25, who remained unmarried despite her beauty and possessions, for she was very demanding and therefore despised all the suitors her father had arranged for her. The princess used to walk among the fields of the plebeians, where she liked to be worshiped and greeted by all. She came to the field where Josiah worked. They all complied with her, except Josiah. The guards immediately arrested him, but the princess signaled that they let him go.

"Tell me, young man, why did not you greet me?"

"Because I'm tired of serving the big guys and not being rewarded for it. Besides, your place is not here. Go back to your castle, where you can pretend that your people are okay and practice their princesses.

Jerusa was impressed by the plebeian's responses. Instead of being angry, she was glad that someone had the guts to say it in her face. Unintentionally, she fell completely in love with him. This was the husband she wanted. He took him to the castle and introduced him to his father.

Over time, he convinced the sovereign to accept him as a son-in-law. The union of Jerusa and Josias was accomplished in the royal hall in a beautiful ceremony with the participation of the main authorities of the region and other kingdoms. Consolidated marriage and trust and friendship of the king, Josiah felt entitled to ask him for a plot of land to fulfill his dream: To establish a vineyard. The King made available the best of his land that was leased: Just Abimael's. Josiah and his royal guard were that the tenant was willing to leave the premises. This did not accept because a contract had been signed which determined that he could use the land for two years. In addition, his vines were almost at harvest point which would bring him a bit Josias (full of himself for being in kingship) did not listen to his arguments and ordered the guards to remove him by force of the place. When it was being arrayed, Abimael exclaimed:

"Is that how you pay the favor I gave you the other day?

Watching him closely, Josiah's heart quickened to recognize in him the man who had once fed him and his mother in the days when he wandered through the villages begging for bread. His proud soul was now completely trampled on, for he who had considered himself an adversary had been saved from misery. At a signal from him, the guards stopped and Josiah approached Abimael, kissing him.

"A thousand pardons, I did not recognize you. You can stay in the vineyard, and you do not even have to pay the rent because you did me a favor and I will give you a generous return.

However, Abimael replied:

"If I had not helped you, I'd be dumped now." He should use his benevolence not only with those who benefit him, but with all the subjects of the kingdom. "We must help the next without condition and without expecting anything in return."

Parable of Creation

At the beginning of time, when life had not yet appeared on earth, the principle (God) prepared the last paraphernalia to begin creation. The great explosion he had caused earlier had left him a little winded. Some gullible readers may wonder: Does God get tired? Certainly. He gets tired of showing us ways, and we do not see, of facilitating our life and of complicating ourselves, of preparing a good plan for our lives, and of rejecting, finally, always giving a new chance to redeem ourselves and revert to old and new mistakes. Is there hope? Depend on us. Let us go back to the parable. The explosion that had originated planets, satellites, stars, asteroids, comets, suns and all the existing mass had taken unexpected proportions because the initial goal was to form a single planet and a single sun. With the exponential multiplication of stars currently forming what we call a universe, unexpected worries came to his mind: How to control and direct such a large, complex and extensive universe How to act without being noticed by his creations How to close the link between the beginning of life and its continuation? Time was no problem at this time, for it had not yet been created. It would be difficult to measure, in current time units, the duration of that period: where drafts and more drafts were torn and, in the planets, that had life, the creation would be composed of two spheres: One spiritual and another material. The spiritual would be invisible from the material would occupy planes and parallel spaces and would have eternal dimensions. The material would be visible, on both planes, would occupy a definite and unchanging position and would have duration determined. One sphere would depend on the other (would be interconnected) forming a complex harmonious and perfect. Genius: This adjective expresses some greatness of the creator. In the following paragraphs, I will highlight some details of this process.

Regarding the spiritual plane, God decided that He would create special beings, full of glory and power, who would act as if they were Him. In different cultures and traditions, they receive different denominations: Angels, evolved and perfect spirits, orishas, messengers, etc. created to rule the universe. One detail: Neither would they have the privilege of knowing it. They would only deduce its existence through manifestations. Then he breathed and created the seven spirits of first greatness: The so-called supreme angels. Their names are eternal and mysterious. Nobody knows them. Together, they represent the creator himself. In the countenance, they bring the perfect and unattainable name. Their bodies have no definite form. They are omnipresent and have the gift of predicting the near future. However, neither were sufficient to control and coordinate the universe in all its functions. Then God breathed and created the hierarchy and along with-it billions of angels according to their castes. This creation continues, some beings of a lesser order would serve as a link between the two spheres: material and spiritual. In some special situations, they would be allowed to transit between the two worlds. The purpose of this would be to restore and maintain the balance between the two planes, the heavenly army was thus created. But material creation was lacking.

Initially, two perfect and indispensable natural laws were created: the life cycle of an organism and the reproductive law. In agreement with the earth, which is a living organism, it was agreed that it would provide the beings with food, shelter, and other necessities for their survival. In return, it would absorb the nutrients at the time of death of the respective organism. In an uninterrupted cycle. Reproduction would allow the perpetuation of the species without the need for successive creations. Other physical laws were also created: the gravitational, the interplanetary movements, the cycle of rains and droughts composing the climate, etc. All this was indispensable to life. Finished this phase, began the application of the sketches of the breeder, turns them into reality. Then God blew out the grass and all the shrubby vegetation necessary for the growth and development of the animals. God was filled with contentment because he saw that all this was excellent. Then God brought forth in the water's innumerable species of fish, of varying sizes and characteristics, interrelated and interdependent. Similar to this, flying creeping beings, animals, insects, microorganisms, bacteria, viruses, fungi, and other indispensable beings to the environment appeared on the earth. All this formed a harmonious complex. God also defined duration, rhythm, and the food chain. This would make the environment healthy and self-sustaining. God blessed them and gave them the instinct to accomplish everything that was programmed. Thereafter, you prepared to carry out your greatest work: The human being. In God's design, this being would be its representation. Gifted with reason and choice, he would organize and dominate the land, making it thrive and fruitful. Making her into a large garden of delights, where she would be happy with her fellow men. It would also be immortal (soul) and would be part of both planes. Among all beings of creation, it would be the most privileged. And so, God did.

Men and women of the most different races emerged: black, white, yellow, etc. Each one in a different part of the earth. God said: Be brothers, multiply, grow, respect, love, change the earth by respecting it and preserving it. See: I gave you vegetation and animals to help you in your needs. I will repay with interest all that you do. I will give the corresponding reward to your deeds. As to the unjust, you will be cut off from your people. And he will have no peace at all. "That said, you have departed." (This was all said to the inmost creature.) The material army was thus completed.

Faced with material creation, there was an episode that had provoked the duality that now exists and consequently the free will of man. Let us see how it happened: There was, in heaven, a beautiful and perfect angel. Being the highest, it had authority and power over all (except God). In time, he became very proud and vain. He was not content to be a servant, and decided to convince a good portion of the angels to rise against the kingdom and to take power. His objective was to reign in the spiritual spheres and material, besides being worshiped as a God. The revolt was discovered in time and its plans failed. The war was armed: On the one hand, Miguel and his angelic servants, defending the sovereignty and the authority of God; malevolent and his followers who wanted to destroy the peace and stability of the kingdom. The universe was completely shaken: The battles were bloody and millions of lives were lost on both sides. The commotion was general. Then the Lord God resolved to intervene to avoid a major catastrophe: He expelled the rebels from the sky plane and threw them into a dark place called abyss. There, they are tormented day and night. Only they are allowed to leave when they are to capture souls. Miguel and his servants were rewarded for their courage and bravery in battle and occupied higher ranks in the administration of the kingdom. They were worthy of the plan in which they were. The two components that act in the universe arose: One beneficial and contributing to the construction of a paradise, another evil and represents the obstacle to the realization of the goal of the first.

Writer's genius. By completing the plot, God created time (existing only in the material sphere) to regulate the actions of the two forces.

The duality created God's plan of action and their respective chiefs. In the evil part was enthroned the supreme angel, who rebelled. Who would then be the head of the kingdom of God? In his plan, God foresaw the construction of a future paradise, where human beings would be free from all kinds of sin. Hunger, despair, doubt, suffering, death, wars and all other evils would no longer exist. However, mankind was corrupted by sin and the consequences were disastrous. Man was no longer worthy to enter into the heavenly plane. What to do? Let us see. By establishing the kingdom of heaven and its respective chief, God had a dual purpose: to organize the spiritual sphere so that there would be no more rebellions, redeeming human sin and thereby opening the doors of paradise. Who would have it? God sought among all his angelic servants, but found no one worthy. The angels were perfect, but did not evolve. They loved them, but not to the point of giving their lives. He became indecision.

After much reflection, a bright idea came to him: He would be himself (only in another form). By being omnipotent, omniscient, omnipresent, and perfect in all attributes, he was the only one capable of carrying out the project. He would save mankind and would restore order and peace in paradise. To achieve this, the angels were informed of this decision and one of them named Gabriel was chosen to be the messenger of the good news to humanity, especially to a young woman named Mary. She would be the mother of God. However, nothing would be forced because she possessed free will. Then the angel approached Mary and exclaimed:

"Get full of grace! You are with you! Behold, he shall bear a son, and shall name him Jesus. This shall be great, and shall be called the son of the highest, and his kingdom shall have no end.

Mary asked, "How will that happen?

The angel answered, "The Holy Spirit will come upon you and cover you with its shadow. Therefore, the saint who will be born of you will be called the son of God. For God, nothing is impossible. Mary said, "Behold the master's servant. Let it be done to me according to your word. Then the angel left her.

By saying yes to the angel, Mary broke with all the bonds of sin and darkness that had plagued humanity since the beginning of creation. It worked to hell and its inhabitants to initiate and reestablish the primacy of good between the two forces. Is the greatest mystery of creation: the author of life itself becoming a character? With this, we can glimpse a little the great love that God nourishes for us. Then the prophecy was fulfilled and Jesus was born from the womb of Mary. Would humanity understand its message?

When Jesus began to preach, he was thirty years old. His time had come. Time to proclaim the good news to men: Forgiveness and remission of sins to those who believed in him. He selected twelve apostles to assist in preaching. He gathered the crowds and told them of his father. Furthermore, he outlined his principal qualities: kindness, omnipotence, justice, wisdom, and the ability to forgive those who repented of their wrongs. He taught us the value of love. And that to experience it, in truth, is to help our neighbor and treat him as we want others to treat us. This is the commandments and the scriptures. In the person of Jesus, God has also revealed to us the purpose that he to build a kingdom of delights, it is necessary primarily to heal our sufferings and anguish. Through him, you have shown us a piece of paradise: A world where all have eternal health and happiness. Death would have no place in a world. Future.

In his incarnation as a human being, God also demonstrated his infinite perfection. Beginning with his origin: Son of a carpenter and born in a stable (among animals). When being born poor, God wanted to teach us that a person's worth is beyond his It is revealed in the acts, in the personality and in the greatness of a heart. Let us see what we are and not what we have. God is primarily the God of the excluded because they are those who generally believe in their existence and are more generous and solidarity. Another great teaching given us by God occurred when he overthrew the cultural structures of the Jews. In presenting him to a prostitute and asking him for his judgment, the Jews expected Jesus to condemn him as if he favored their petty convictions and inferior judgments. Jesus denied this. Jesus recognized in the woman a heart and disposition of never found in women who claimed to be respectful. She was worth more than the others. From that day on, the prostitute followed him and discovered that her body was too precious to be given to anyone. Jesus changed his life: He went, the only one not to condemn it and to believe in its character and dignity. A being without prejudices (sex, race, color, social class, sexual orientation, etc.) was that the wonderful God that Jesus revealed to us. This is evidenced in the choice of the twelve apostles: A fisherman, a tax collector, etc. Standards that were simply ignored and rejected by the current system.

The preaching of Jesus lasted three years. In this period, he gathered followers and propagated the good news of the kingdom. Many rejected him, but this did not give up. His plan was not terrestrial: It was something that encompassed both spheres. He said: My kingdom is not of this world. The earth was not prepared for such a radical change. Petty feelings and fear were still infiltrating the human soul, preventing the realization of the plan. In the future world, this would be possible. Before that, however, the stain of sin (what separated man from the sky plane) could be erased. How would this be done? Let's go back a bit in history. The Jewish priests offered small sacrifices to Yahweh, the God of the Exodus, to redeem the sin of the people and their own. With each new error, more sacrifices were needed. For Yahweh, life was sacred, and he was not completely content with these rituals. Then he decided: A perpetual sacrifice would be performed to abolish the former. The victim to be slain was his son Jesus, for he was the only perfect human on earth. And so, it was done. The Son of Man was crucified and thereby freed us from the bonds of sin. Henceforth, those who believe in his name and follow his teachings will have eternal life and happiness guaranteed in this and another plan. He is the perfect model of man that God has given us to be followed. Whomever they attain will be called also children of God and will take place guaranteed in the future world.

After the death and crucifixion of Jesus, God went back to the heavens to rewrite his plans. In his stay on earth, he realized how much suffering brings dualism: Famines, wars, injustices, hypocrisy, etc. In the new world, only the good and its followers will remain. Those who opt for the other component, the evil one, will be excluded from this group. With this, paradise will be concretely established on the physical plane.

The kingdom

Behold, the kingdom of the heavens may be compared to a virgin who chooses a husband among many suitors. Everyone tries to impress her by offering all sorts of dowries, but she does not let herself be carried away. She values them by the qualities of each one, and what is true is to show true love to one's neighbor. Many try to enter through this door, but few are chosen.

The true victory

There were two farmers in Ancient Greece. They were neighbors of the land and prepared the land, fertilized the plants, planted the seeds precisely in the same period. The climate was favorable because it provided sun and rain at the right time. With this, the plantations fruited, which left both happy. However, an overwhelming pest (birds and grasshoppers) massively attacked one of the plantations. The owner was in a rush and used of several devices to expel the invaders. The parasites did not give up and fought for the easy food until the end. When the owner managed to exterminate them, all his work had already been wasted because the damage in the plantation was shown irreversible. Resounding of satisfaction, he called his neighbor and said,

"Compadre, I managed to win the fight! Destroy those plagues!

"Heck, you lost!" While you were worried about driving them out, I reaped the fruits of my labor, and I did not mind losing a few feet of the crop I sowed, for some of these pests also attacked my plantation. If you had done the same, there would be no such thing as injury.

"And now, my friend, what do I do?"

"Do not worry. You will not starve because I will share what I have gathered with you. The important thing is to learn that the true winner is not the one who wins the fight, but the one who knows how to avoid it without harming himself.

The merchant and the consumer

Gabriel was a prosperous merchant of Garanhuns. He once dispatched a strange consumer. Let's see how the dialogue happened.

"I want the merchandise x. How much?

"Six reais and thirty-four cents. Want only a unit?

"Yes. Only one.

"Here it is. (Delivering the product)

The stranger handed him a ten-dollar bill. Strangely enough, the merchant did not have enough money to give him the right change. He returned only three reais and sixty cents. The merchant said:

"Six cents are missing. If you want to wait, I'll give you the rest somehow. I do not have five and one cent coins in the box."

"You can keep the six cents. I do not want them. To succeed in life, it takes six things: Respect, commitment, solidarity, understanding, cunning, and love of neighbor. Practice them, and the six cents will multiply indefinitely. Remember: Never despise the five and one cent coins because they together make up billions, and great will be the fortune of those who understand this maxim: Unity makes the force.

The two shepherds

Sidrac and Abdênago were shepherds from the region of the Galileans. The two led their herds together, differentiated only by a superficial mark on the skin of the sheep. One day, at sundown, Abdênago noticed the lack of one of his sheep in counting them. Strangely, he decided to question Sidrac.

"One of my sheep is missing. Did you leave it behind, or did it die?

"I was taking courage to give you the bad news: When we were eating, a starving lion took advantage of our absence and ate one of the sheep. I found out why I found this (showing a carcass). Precisely, it was the one that is missing."

"How unlucky!" Especially because he chose mine. Next time, we will be more careful in order not to have any more damage."

After some time, again, Abdênago realized the lack of one of his sheep. Sidrac asked.

"One of my sheep is missing. Was it the lion that devoured them?

"Not this time. When you left to meet your needs, I was approached by two desert merchants who surrendered and took the sheep. I tried to follow them, but it was useless. It was just yours.

"" How unlucky!" Next time, I will try to satisfy my needs at home.

A while later, again, Abdênago found one of his sheep missing. Sidrac asked.

"One of my sheep is missing. Were they the merchants who stole it?

"Not this time. A beautiful maiden led by an old man marveled at a copy of his and begged me to present it. I did not resist his talents and rewarded him.

"She had to choose mine. So, I've already taken two.

Analyzing some of Sidrac's sheep, he realized that the marks had disappeared, which made it impossible to identify them. He decided to question Sidrac.

"How do you know the three sheep were mine?" There is no mark that distinguishes them.

"They were yours. I assure you, therefore, that I was present at all times.

"Thief! You gave yourself up. If he was, he could have stopped them from leaving. You did not avoid it because you stole them yourself. Now you have to return them, or I will report them to the authorities.

"Calm down, Abdênago. I will return them. I want to avoid being arrested.

Furthermore, I thought you were my friend. From today, I will lead my flock alone. Much better, would I be if I were alone?

The rich boy and the poor boy

Ricardo and Rafael studied in the same series in an educational establishment of high social level. Ricardo was the son of businessmen and lived in the central part of the city in a beautiful mansion. Rafael was the son of domestic servants and resided in a hotel on the outskirts of the city. He had been given a scholarship because of the great grades he had earned.

They were partners and friends at school. One day, Ricardo invited Rafael to spend a weekend at his house. He accepted and was impressed when he arrived. The friend had everything a child wanted to have in material terms. Ricardo showed his friend his room with all his toys and his personal belongings. This caused some jealousy in Rafael. They spent about an hour playing together in the room and then decided to go out for some fresh air. Rafael drew subject:

"I wanted to live in a house like this because here has everything a child needs: Toys, space for leisure, stewardship. You must be pleased, should not you?

Ricardo looked at himself and was pensive and silent. Rafael insisted:

"Tell me, you have everything you want, do not you?

"On the one hand, I have: Everything that money can buy. On the other hand, I need other things that are not attainable in money: Understanding, love and friendship. My parents dictate me inflexible rules that I have to they do not blink and most of the time they live working. They do not have time to give me affection, and so I feel closer to my employees. Did you see my toys? Nothing is worth if I do not have someone to share them. Before of you coming, they were thrown into a corner and did not call my attention.

Rafael was moved and realized that he had made a mistake in making that comment. After all, happiness is not found in material goods. Despite being poor, he lived in a well-built family: He had received a proper education with values of character that an honest person must have; The dialogue was open with his parents whenever there was any doubt; The love and affection he received from his relatives helped him to forget the poverty in which he lived. He took the floor:

"Sorry, I did not know. You were transparent to have happiness in your hands. Anyway, know that you have a friend in me, even though you do not belong in your social circle."

The two embraced and made a covenant of eternal friendship.

The Alien and the Earth man

João Pereira was a rural worker who worked on a farm. One night at night he saw a lightness around the sheepfold. He decided to investigate because he could be a thief. As he approached, he was amazed at what he saw: A luminous circular object and next to it something like a man. The stranger had crouched and caressed the sheep. Although he was intimidated about the strange creature, he decided to act because he could not allow him to steal the sheep from the boss. Cried out:

"Do not touch those sheep!" They do not belong to you.

The alien sensed the presence of the human and adjusted his language. He had to respond to that.

"What's wrong with touching them? They did not complain about my caresses. They do not belong to anyone.

"Not at all. My boss owns them. He bought them from a merchant in the city.

"It was him. The only owner of them is the environment: It is they who will consume them at the end of their existence.

"You can see that you're not from here. In this world, beings who have intelligence is the boss. Look at my situation: I work all day, and occasionally, I work at night. While I'm here, my boss snores into a beautiful bed. What to do? The only thing is to accept.

"So, you think of yourself as an intelligent life. I did not realize that. How can intelligent life exist on a planet that is about to collapse? The life force of your planet is being affected by your irrational practices: Deforestation, mining, pollution, excessive hunting and fishing, etc. Tell me, what are you going to do when your power supplies run out? How will your descendants survive? All this, why? Because of the meager metal you call money. I assure you: In the future, nothing will remain. Then the money will have no value.

"It is true. I feel that the earth produces less and less. She looks tired. But what to do? How to reverse this?

"Is easy. Be simple like these sheep. They graze, drink, reproduce according to the rhythm of nature. You should do the same: Treat nature with respect and with the care, it deserves. Then you will survive.

The ship opened, and the stranger flew toward his entrance. In less than two seconds, the ship disappeared from the view of the worker.

He commented:

"Only words. Who would listen to them? The sovereigns of industrialized nations would never give up the financial resources that nature offers them. They only care about the growth of the economy of their respective countries. Although the consequences that the alien cited in the future are inevitable. There will be no stone left on this planet.

The Labyrinth

Once upon a time, in a distant kingdom, a princess and a prince loved each other. The wedding was set to take place in about three months, and the joy was general. The King was already old and would deliver the throne to the prince in the day of the wedding. Unfortunately, fate did not allow this, and he died before. The throne was provisionally delivered to the king's counselor (Magno) because the royal heirs were not of age. The short time in power was enough to fill him with pride, and Magno decided to expel the prince of the palace and threw the princess in a jail. His objective was to avoid the union of the two to dominate the kingdom.

Magno, besides being a counselor, was a skilled sorcerer. By expelling the prince of the kingdom, he created an immense labyrinth around the royal palace so that no one would strike him. Whoever looked at him had the false impression that he had no entrance or exit. Being released from the royal palace, the prince gathered his last forces to return and rescue the princess. Fitted with sword and staff, went to the labyrinth. His love was all concentrated in the strength of his fists and in his arms. The first blow which he delivered was over the labyrinth, and with this, he got an entry. He began to walk the narrow paths between the walls of the labyrinth, but no matter how hard he tried, he could not find the exit. During 3 hours, he wandered and uselessly. Decided to stay where he was lying on the ground. Observing the sky, he noticed something curious: Some birds flew towards the palace and then returned to the point where he was. He decided to risk: I would follow them in his flight. He quickly accompanied the bird on its way and the exit opened in front of him. With a beautiful push, he opened the door of the palace and found Magno seated on the throne. He approached and with the staff, the prince the and with a blow of the sword cut off his head. Instinctively, the labyrinth disappeared and the rails that held the princess as well. The two embraced and kissed each other, promising eternal love. Together with all his kingdom, they were happy forever.

The Game of Life

David and Hélio were two very close brothers. Recently, they had completed the technical vocational training course in a renowned federal institution. Being a high level, the course provided them with a paid internship in a large company. Their abilities would be observed and put to the test in that period. In a second moment, only the most capable would remain in the company as an effective employee.

From childhood, despite being united, the two fought the attention of the parents: Each one wanted to be the favorite like, for example, the distribution of toys at Christmas and when their mother was going to tell a story. In social relations (friends in common) wanted to always be the leaders of the group and to have more prominence in discussions of subjects of interest. In addition, at the school where they studied, competed to reach the best grades. When they entered puberty, they began to bet who would win more girlfriends. In short, their lives were entwined with innumerable disputes over time. The time had come for them to work and win professional success, and again they would compete against each other. This time, it would not be easy.

The internships began, and the two devoted themselves intensely to get a good performance and impress the supervisors. Several tests were carried out, but none of them stood out enough to be considered the owner of the vacancy. Finally, it was decided that the two would be submitted to a final test. This would be decisive relates their permanence in the company. David, the most astute, secretly defrauded the work of his brother Hélio. In his vision, in war, in work and in love everything is worth. Get the job done, and Helio realized that something was wrong with his. Finished giving up and went to help his brother David who was in trouble. The two finished work together according to the supervisor. Satisfied, he applauded and said:

"The decision I made regarding your permanence in the company was based on an attentive observation of the behavior of the two during the internship. I ended up deciding for Helio because he demonstrated beyond creative competence, teamwork, and solidarity. As for you, David, selfishness and competition blinded you. For your petty goals, you discarded your mate. Learn a lesson to get a decent job and succeed in life: "Not everything is valid in a dispute".

The Fish and the Star

In the submerged world, in the water bicycles, there were innumerable shoals of fish of various species. One of these shoals lived in great depth, at the end of the sea. Belonging to him was an exceptional fish: He was the only one of his schools without a sexual partner. Passion had not hit her heart and her guts. Without love, she could not relate to anyone. Occasionally, he did not even understand his attitudes: He wanted to love, to procreate, but he was not attracted to anyone. "He was a stranger in his shoal."

At the same time, in the firmament, where there are infinite quantities of stars forming what is called the universe, there was a special one: a star that enchanted everyone and imposed respect for its flashing light. However, she could not love and be loved. For one reason or another, she and the other stars could not understand each other.

One night, the fish, uneasy on the seabed, out of curiosity decided to emerge to see for the first time the sky crowned with stars. The time he had was only one second. As he emerged, he observed that strange combination of dots in his masterly dispersion. His sea-eyes fixed themselves on a splendid star that was special among all of them. His heart flashed, and his soul was struck by the weapon of the cupid God. Concomitantly, in heaven, the star fixed her gaze under the waters and saw a small being. What a lovely creature! She exclaimed. Her light shone with a special intensity to discover something that caught her attention. This moment lasted a short time, but was enough to produce a great impact.

Day after day, after night, the meetings were repeated and with that, a great love was being solidified. Over time, this became a suffering because the two lovers could not consolidate this relationship by the distance and incompatibility of environments. In addition, they feared for the incomprehension of their fellow men. Despite this, both tried to solve this situation: The star went to speak with the Star-king of its galaxy to ask permission to date the fish. The Star-king replied: "you are a star, full of light and brightness. You cannot date a fish. Look for another star to date. "" I love you, "replied the star." You cannot, "the Star-King reporter replied uncompromisingly." At sea, the fish went to consult the king of the fish to explain their desires. Heaven to make love with a star! "The king of the fish answered," He cannot. You are a fish, so find another female fish to date. Their anguish increased: How can we concretely achieve the feeling between the two? They wanted to touch, hug, kiss. But how to overcome such difficulties? Faced with this, the Earth (who watched everything) decided to take sides. When the two of them again looked at each other, the earth communicated: "Do you want to love yourself?" She asked. I can help you. As? He inquired about the star and the fish.

"At midnight, I have the right to make a request to the creator. This time, I will ask for the communion between you. I have observed them all this time and I do not think the suffering they carry is just. Let it be for God, love, nothing is impossible., you will be the first to leave its habitat. You will reach the edge of the surface, where I will cover you with my mud and give you a terrestrial body. You will be called a man, and you will dominate all the beings of the surface. Heaven and will unite with man. They must be united because they love each other. Their light will illuminate the body, giving it a spirit. When they become one, the love God will take a rib from the man and form his body. You will have a mark on the body. In man, this mark will be called Adam's apple and will represent the refusal of the gods of their respective habitats. In the woman, the mark will be called breasts and will represent the union of the two and the force of love. He will feed his fruit so that they may be strong, as is the feeling of you. For they have loved each other without reserve, they will also be called "sons of God the love" as well as their fruits. In the end, your body will die, but love will not. Your spirits will rise to the heavens and there they will know the God that created them and will be united to him because he is also the love.

The Invisible Companion

In ancient Baghdad, there was a merchant named Issachar. To stock his tent and those of some friends many times through the desert. In all these journeys he seldom met anyone on the road because the desert was a dry and dangerous place. On a day of exception, he met a certain man who appeared to be a peasant. He stopped his dromedary and asked for water. The merchant gently yielded a little, though it was a rare liquid. The man, after drinking exhaustively, surrendered him by stealing all his merchandise.

The person's name was Aramis. A good part of the merchandise he stole would help him with the expenses of his house. The rest would use to buy presents and would offer to the priests of his temple. And so, he did. He attended the temple and met a master of his religion. He promptly gave her some donations. The master was impressed by the greatness of these gifts and immediately suspected him as a simple peasant. He decided to ask:

"How did you get such gifts?"

"I worked hard this year and that's why I got them, he replied.

The jerk's voice did not come out and denounced it. The master replied:

"I do not accept these offerings. They are impure. Return them to the owner immediately.

The peasant was perplexed by the cunning of the master.

"How do you know they are not mine? I was alone when I committed the crime, "he observed.

"Your mistake. You were not alone. His conscience accompanied him all the time and betrayed him, replied the master.

The Drunk And the conscious

Henrique was a young man of high social class. However, he was not happy about this condition. One of the reasons was that he felt abandoned by his parents who gave him from birth to the care of a nanny, and so he did not feel loved by in his childhood he had always been a troubled child, and in his youth, he became a revolted young man. One example of this is that he stopped attending college to amuse himself in public and private parties.

On these occasions, he eventually found his way to drugs such as marijuana, tobacco, cocaine, and alcohol. In a way, drugs were a way to catch the attention of parents, but even that was not enough to wake them up.

Once he was in a drug-taking bar when he fell unconscious. One of his relatives arrived and began beating him and cursing him, and at that moment one of the members of an NGO that helps young drug addicts was present and revolted with the attitude of the familiar. He got up from the table where he was and gently held Henry and woke him up. The stranger said:

"You're drunk, who does not realize that this boy needs help." Drunk of prejudice and ignorance!

With this, Henrique declared:

"I'm drunk and even then, I understand that my true family is this man because he cared for me unlike you who only criticized me.

The antiquarian

Ti Juan was a small merchant from China. On his bench, he marketed various trinkets that were considered sacred to him. Under the circumstances, he was forced to sell them. On one of these occasions, a parliamentarian approached his small tent with the purpose of buying a piece for his residence. On his arrival, he immediately pointed to a sculpture of a woman studded with thorns and adorned with a golden crown. He began to negotiate.

"I want that piece. How much?

Ti Juan paled and murmured in annoyance:

"It is not for sale. It's a piece of sentimental value.

The parliamentarian replied:

"I pay well. I offer you a million dollars for that piece.

"Not for a billion, I see it. No business.

Meanwhile, a small peasant appeared, holding a clay sculpture in his hand.

"Sir, could you get this piece? I did it myself.

The merchant examined it and began to negotiate his purchase.

"Money, I do not have, but I can offer something in return. How about an appetizer?

"No way. I exchange it for that piece (pointing to the sculpture intended by the parliamentarian).

"Did you sleep, boy? Do you know the value of that piece? Know that she belonged to a legendary princess of ancient Mesopotamia.

"And? The exchange will be more favorable to you than to me.

"Because?

"My work is splendid and modern, while your work translates suffering and permeates the environment of bad luck. As one old saying goes: "Take old things out of your trunk and replace them with new ones."

The merchant thought for a moment, and then he decided:

"You can take it. In recent times, it only brought me headache. Starting today, I will recycle my trade: I will sell old and new objects that convey good aspects. Enjoy it and keep shining your gifts. "Our works have to be seen by all".

The Librarian

Cesar had worked as a librarian in a large library for over ten years. He was a great connoisseur of the collection of books that constituted it. Once a young man approached him and asked,

"Could you recommend a good book?"

He replied:

"I'll bring some, and you'll choose."

In a short time, it came crammed with books from the main bookshelf and placed them randomly on a table. There were books of all sizes and peculiarities. César invited:

"Let's go. Choose what pleases you most.

The young man handled them and watched them closely. Finally, it was decided:

"I want this one: It is much bigger than the others and has a beautiful cover. Here must be an impressive and thought-provoking story.

Caesar laughed and said,

"Your mistake. See this little book I'm handling? I read it and believe it: It is more interesting than this book you chose. In these few pages, there is much more content you can imagine. You see: The cover and size of the book does not define them. "It is only when we read that we know its true value."

Then the young man put down the book in his hands and concluded:

"That's right. I will take this minor because I trust in his analysis. On the way back, I will tell you my opinion of him.

The two of them said goodbye, and they would meet again a fortnight later. At the reunion, the librarian greeted him kindly and promptly inquired:

"What's up? Like or dislike the book?

"I loved it. Its content is really impressive: It tells the personal story of a young man who finds in a cave the last hope of fulfilling his dreams. The title is all about: "Opposing forces: The mystery of the grotto". Whoever buys it will not regret it, it is very intriguing and instructive.

"Where did you like the most?

"From the experience in the cave and how the main character became the seer."

"I do not agree. In my opinion, the part after the view is the most interesting. But I respect your opinion.

"I respect you, too." With you, I have learned that the judgment we make about something or someone is extremely partial and subjective. Thanks for the lesson.

Forewarned and reckless

Rosinha and Frufru were two homosexuals who were prostituting themselves. Every night, they stood on the edge of a corner and offered their services to anyone who passed by. Rosinha was ethical because she only accepted the relationship if the man were single and had a condom. Frufru already had no such concern.

A night, Frufru fainted in the middle of the avenue. Her friend Rosinha was careful to call the ambulance to help her. Because of her sexual conduct, she underwent several tests and one of them found that Frufru was carrying the HIV virus. Now she was part of the crowd that was condemned to die prematurely. After she returned to her nights, she would be an instrument of death for other people. Thus, initiating a new cycle of disease.

Despite all Campaigns, HIV continues to spread rapidly. He does not choose race, creed, sexual choice or social origin. Everyone is at risk of being infected and prevention is the best and only way to stop this epidemic. Do not do like Frufru, but like Rosinha: Prevent yourself, take care, love yourself.

The key

Elias was a retired key ring from the interior of Pernambuco. Despite his fixed salary, he used to practice his old errand. One of those times, she went to see a lady who had been anxiously bound to have lost the key to her apartment door. He took his old car in his garage and along with it a bunch of keys of the most varied types and shapes. Certainly, one of them would open the door of the said lady.

Arriving at the destination, she greeted her client and asked her to calm down as she would solve the problem. Repeatedly, the woman pronounced:

"Open the door. I have something important to do. Strive.

The key chain, somewhat annoyed by the pressure and insistence of the lady, tried several keys until she could open the door. The woman sighed with relief:

"You still have. Thank you! Here is your payment (handing you some notes). Is the tip included. When I'm in trouble again, can I call you?

"Of course, yes. However, it is not necessary to be so distressed. When a door is closed to us, God (in His mercy) always gives us an alternative: Another key, another entrance, a new path. So do not worry unnecessarily.

That said, the key chain said goodbye and headed for his car. Before entering, he heard a cry from the woman and turned to her.

"Tell me, sir, is there a key to opening someone's heart?"

"I do not know or possess. But often, it is we who close the door of our hearts. Tip: Do not try to force it open by using multiple keys. Rather, open your door and shine securely and sincerely all your attitudes and feelings. This is enough to conquer the other in all its fullness.

"Thank you for the advice. The key was in front of me and I did not notice.

"To unlock doors in life requires dedication, honesty and humility."

The frog and the butterfly

There was a frog and a butterfly in a certain habitat. Both liked to walk: The butterfly, to show its stunning beauty and arrogance; the frog, to look for food. Once they met and were amazed. The butterfly could not contain itself and asked:

"Why did God create such a freak? Only the beautiful should exist. Poor creature, why do not you commit suicide?

"No, my lady. This is not necessary. I feel as good as you. The ugly does not exist in nature, but the different. Know that I have utility in the ecosystem: I am an important pest reducer. In addition, I bring prosperity and hope. While the lady with her beauty does not perform an important mister. In fact, it can even cause damage to some living beings. What you have of beautiful on the outside is rotten inside because you do not know what respect is. You should be ashamed of it.

At the toad's reply, the butterfly fell silent and immediately withdrew. Her empire was broken and she never criticized anyone again. After the lesson, he remembered the time when he was a horrible caterpillar and was not less important to God.

An Important Lesson

In Greece, there was an important sage famous throughout the region. He was considered thus for solving complicated cases. His knowledge and wisdom came from a single source: The books that comprised his extensive library. In time, it was convinced that it arrived at a high level of intellectuality and therefore decided to virtually isolate himself from the world. The only contact that remained as a real world were the attendance sessions that took place once a week. In his remaining time, he took care of the house and practiced meditation beyond reading of new books.

Once, in one of the attendance sessions, he was visited by a young man from a nearby village. Like the others, he walked in properly, bowed and sat down beside her. He threw the following challenge to the wise:

"Master, what is the true meaning of the word love?

"Love is a subtle way to turn a blind eye to reality, and it becomes a complete surrender to a person without measuring the consequences. The one who loves feels weak, insecure and lacking in the company of one who loves himself.

"I understand. Have you ever loved?

"No, I've never. I was too busy in my quest for knowledge, and besides loving, it hampers evolution toward infinity.

"Then your knowledge has no foundation. Practice cannot be dissociated from theory. On what is it based to qualify the sentiment complex love?

"In my studies. I have already researched this topic in countless records. With that, I drew my own conclusions.

"Master, do you really believe that this is enough? In the registers you have access are engraved impressions and opinions of others with characteristics and personalities different from yours. Basement in them to conceptualize love makes your opinion extremely superficial. In fact, there is no fixed concept for this and I have had an experience that makes me ensure that what I felt is nothing like its definition. In my opinion, loving is to open your eyes to a new reality full of colors and meaning and beyond all is surely a complete and perfect evolution that encompasses two worlds. Who loves feels strong even in difficult times and is able to rely on the good nature of the other? In short, to love is to live each day without escaping from problems When you love, what seems like an obstacle can be seen as an experience and this is something that you will not discover in any book because it is part of the practice. It is not here, between four walls, that you it will evolve and find peace because it is built within ourselves and this is possible only if we open our feelings to each other and to the world every day. To denounce this is to lose the most important part of life.

The master, faced with the apprentice's response, was stunned and did not know what to say. The contest put to the ground all the knowledge that he supposed to possess and now had no arguments. Sitting in his chair as if on a throne, he did not realize that the sun was rising and falling as he closed his world. Humbly, he rose from his altar and answered the young man,

"You are the true master. I am not worthy to be called so. You have shown me how limited my wisdom and my knowledge is. Are you seeing these books? (Pointing to your immense library). I will give you all my poor countrymen. I will leave this enclosure and I will go around the world in search of true knowledge: Experience. As for you, come. I will give you my throne and my authority and therefore you will be exalted by kings and tycoons and will mark his name in history.

The young man replied:

"I do not want to, because I'm not interested in power or ostentation. My only goal is to achieve something similar to what is called happiness. Wisdom does not belong to me, nor is I willing to try to find it. Before God, there is no wise, therefore, our sciences and investigations are considered madness for him. In truth, the creator is the true sage, and the throne, power, kindness, and authority are inherent in all righteousness.

Parable of life

Life is a great field where numerous and diverse species of seeds are sown. Some rot because they are stony, flowing, dry or because they are not watered correctly. Other's fruit and become trees full of branches and fruits because they are in and how to understand the great mystery of creation and be an agent of the will of God if we do not even know it to understand its will and its project?

In a large forest in Brazil, there were two woodcutters: Both were married and had children. They lived in nearby huts and lived from the extraction of the natural resources that the habitat provided. They were called John and Peter. John and his sons worked from the north side of their hut, over thirty acres. João had learned from his father to manage the forest: He was an adept at selective collection, a way of deforesting without damage to nature. The larger and wider trees were felled, being careful that in the fall it did not harm the neighboring trees. collection was periodic, so as not to affect the rhythm and natural stock of the forest. So, would have plenty of wood as long as he lived. He remade what he had learned from his father to his children. In hunting and fishing, he respected spawning and the period of reproduction thus contributing to avoid subsequent extinctions of species. Each day, he hunted and fished just enough for his survival and his family. He never killed the animals for sport and taught his children to do the same. He also used a small space of three where he sowed beans, corn, pumpkin, watermelon and roots and seedlings of other plants. His cultivation was different from the others: He never practiced burning to clear the land because he that this practice would exhaust the nutrients of the soil and the land would soon become infertile. He also taught his children. In addition to these practices, he had learned to respect, love and value his family, the forest and its ecosystems, his county, state and country. From a small one, he had noticed that everything is interconnected as in a great spider's web. If he cut some of these wires, everything would be harmed (including him). He felt an integral part of nature and not owner of it. He did not know God but believed in his existence and learned to discover his will through the creatures themselves. He was happy and taught everyone how to hit it mainly the children who were his greatest pride and treasure. They would be powerful trees, with abundant branches and fully integrated at will of a higher being.

Pedro was John's neighbor. He and his sons worked on the south side of their hut on an area of sixty hectares. Pedro had learned not to respect the forest: He collected his resources in a disorderly and disorganized way (all trees of commercial value They were used by aggressive collection devices that destroyed everything around them. He always said to himself: When there is a shortage of wood here, I will look elsewhere (as if the wood were never finished). In the fishery, he superexploited the species of greater importance and did not respect the spawn even with the incentives of the government. The profit for him was more important. He was adept of capitalism. In hunting, besides killing for his sustenance and for the sales, he liked to scare the animals and harm them by sport. In his conscience, he thought that he owned all that and acted in whatever way he liked. He also taught his sons. burned to not have much work. When the ground was exhausted, he would look for another and repeat the same error. He taught his children to act in the same way. Regarding religion, he did not believe in God. For him, life was only a form of exploitation of the strongest over the weakest. Your children would be barren trees because we are usually what we learn.

Unfortunately, what is seen is a generalized increase of Pedros in that country. With the increasing destruction of our resources, what we have left? We have destroyed the Atlantic Forest, the pine forest and many other agglomerations of raw forest. We pollute rivers, our air, we have already reduced the number of living species. Similar to João are few and rare. The ones that act in this way are called idiots. We are idiots because we respect life and we oppose the adopted model of production, model globalized. However, we are worthy and models of good trees that produce, fruit, grow and give a good shadow to those who seek them. This is what God wants.

3.18-The Fisherman And the fish

In the Northeast, a river. This river was the most important in the region because it was a breeding ground for countless species of fish and because it possessed one of the most limpid and potable waters of the semiarid. Most of the rivers of this region, it dried. In this period, most of the population moved in search of better conditions of life. However, in a time of such a riverbank was therefore believed in the strength of the earth although she is tired and to be barren. He dreamed of a day when the desert would be blessed and had the conditions to give its inhabitants a decent life. Although this was only a dream.

With every passing day, hunger was tightening and thirst as well. The little water available was fiercely disputed by people and animals. As the situation worsened, the fisherman decided to dig his own well. As he dug, his mind flew in innumerable thoughts about the abundance he had: the numerous fish he fished, the fat animals he was able to slaughter, and the gentle breeze that was now replaced by a strong, burning, suffocating heat. He finally finished and what was his surprise when he found a small school of live fish, limpid, fat and healthy. He asked the fish,

"How did you survive the dry season?"

"Simple. We were parched and sun-trapped in a small pool of water that dried faster and faster. Death was coming when we realized that we were close to one of the holes you had made the previous summer. One by one we managed to jump into the hole and reach the remaining water. There is always an alternative to our problems. Sometimes, just think a little and look aside we solve them. The worst would be to accommodate us without trying. We would be dead now. When it gets too full, water will flood this place and life will begin again.

"Your attitude was wise. However, I am obliged by circumstances to eat them. In respect to the river, I will let one of you survive. It will guarantee a sufficient harvest of fish for the next year.

Then he picked them up and took them home. The fish cried for their lives, but he did not listen. The hunger and despair of his children spoke louder. "The problems and goals of others are second to ours," and "the strongest makes use of its strength."

4-Conclusion

Kingdom and Wisdom's Parables was written with the aim of passing on knowledge to readers in general. I hope I have achieved the goal and made the reader better as a human being.

As for the aspect of the book, it can be classified as a book of parables on the general themes Kingdom of God and Wisdom. To write them I have inspired myself in the sea of wisdom of the creator and with me he has the merit of the book. I hope I have contributed to the two general aspects mentioned above. Thanks for the attention, readers. A hug and we meet in the next book.

The End

www.ingramcontent.com/pod-product-compliance
Lightning Source LLC
LaVergne TN
LVHW020443080526
838202LV00055B/5318